SWINGING ON A STAR

Swinging

ON A

Star

DAVID

TRINIDAD

Turtle Point Press

BROOKLYN, NEW YORK

Requests for permission to make copies of
any part of the work should be sent to:

TURTLE POINT PRESS
208 Java Street, 5th Floor
Brooklyn, NY 11222
www.turtlepointpress.com

Library of Congress Cataloging-in-Publication Data
is available from the publisher upon request

Design by Quemadura

ISBN 978-1-933527-97-0
Printed in the United States of America

Acknowledgments: *Columbia Poetry Review*,
Denver Quarterly, *Poem-a-Day* (Academy of
American Poets), *PoetryNow* (Poetry Foundation).

CONTENTS

1. Bedrock at Night

2. Ode to Buddy Holly

BEDROCK AT NIGHT

To be one such one—for one night only.
To be singled out
for this brief distinction

and fly first class (on miles),
wear black tie, walk red carpet.
To be met with smiles

and camera-flash
and then be asked,
by a stringer,
"Who are you?"

"A poet? What's it
like to be that?"

One only exists
when being photographed.
One fawns all over

the aged activist—
infirm but famous.
One hungers for
the elusive hors d'oeuvres.

One meets one:
an Oscar winner
who looks great—for 83.
His secret: carrot juice.

One finds
one has nothing
to say.

SOMETHING DEEP IN ME

lacks courage
to come forth

unlike the lake
ruffling acres of teal silk
or the sky above it

that dissipates
to a thin smear of grayish blue
allowing the cream-colored truth

to streak through

Not all sins
can be confessed

Must keep some secrets
buried

where words
won't reach

THE AFTERLIFE OF FAME

                        is dark
a neglected mansion

with vanishing court
rats in the empty pool

and antiquated actress
languishing

as ghost of her famous self
flickers in the projector's beam

or framed in silver
haunts every room

Face unrecognizable?
Name forgotten?

O float me to Oblivion
in my swan bed

with my bandaged wrists
and doors shorn of locks

with swirl of my cigarette smoke
and glitter of my jewels

and silent flutter
of my weightless tulle

P IS FOR PAGODA

A poodle sits on a pumpkin
playing the piano

A Persian prince
sits on a pile
of purple and pink pillows
feeding a peacock
pie

What do you see beginning with P?

Parasol
Powder puff
Pigtail
Plum

A penguin pens a puzzle

The prince puffs a pipe
sports pearls

WHEN POETS APPEAR IN DREAMS

Sitting with Jean Valentine and Timothy Liu

on my parents' brown plaid '70s sofa
in the family room
of my childhood home.

Timothy had written something
and signed his name, in blue ink,
on the wall, next to a photograph of himself.

"You may have started a tradition,"
I told him.

We laughed quietly at that.

I had squeezed his calf
affectionately
when he cozied up on the sofa
between Jean and me.

Jean's head was shaved.
A guest of my parents,
she was staying in a room
off of the family room.

(In real life this room didn't exist.)

The door to the room
was half open
and I could see
that it was oddly aglow.

was in a pink
tulip with
her lover—
were they bees?

M M

about to slip
from this world
into the next

skin glistening

fresh from her
closed-set skinny-dip

in the blue Hollywood pool

of forgetfulness

NATE

       suffered
from insomnia. (He was a big pot-smoker.)

His mother would wake up
in the middle of the night

and find him in the kitchen
making a sandwich.
One night she found him

standing outside in the rain.
Standing in the rain

red hair wet, arms outstretched
enjoying it

amazed by it—
he was alive (and would die young)

in the rain in the middle of the night.

LEE ANN BROWN

is leading a graduate
poetry workshop
in my dream

I sit in on it

Room dimly lit

Students—
about half
a dozen
in a semicircle—
seem content

I ask if
Lee Ann has
sung any of
her poems
to them

She shakes
her head no

smiles shyly

Her thick hair
tied in back
is dyed
a vivid red—

no, orange

the color
of a Creamsicle

in white silk,
wrapped in folded-over
tissue like
a 1940s/1950s doll
in a box,
an angel or bride doll.

Thank you, Anne,
for visiting my dream.

BEDROCK AT NIGHT

Safe in their round granite houses
from stegosaurus and snaggletooth
the cavepeople sleep

The caveman dreams
of bowling strikes
with a big stone ball

The cavewoman beside him
dreams of a new bone
for her hair

Outside their round bedroom window
palm trees and animal tools
are still

Dinosaur mower and scissor-beaked
hedge clippers
snooze together on the lawn

Even the bird car horn
on the footmobile in the garage
snores three cartoon Z's

The little suburb of Bedrock
deep in its
Stone Age sleep

While above
stars big as boulders
sparkle

And the full moon
biggest and roundest rock of all
presides

Over the blue prehistoric night

NO POEM CAN SAVE YOU

when your spouse
unexpectedly dies
in the middle of the night

when your dog
or cat is gone

when your parents disappoint you

when your children disappoint you

when your husband
leaves you
for a younger
version of yourself

when your best friend
betrays you
by siding

with the one person
who has hurt you
the most

when

MAUVE ODE

Love was more
romantic in the
1960s: a boy could
grow his hair long
& wear striped
pants & a purple
velvet jacket with
ruffled cuffs &
not fear ridicule
while a girl (not
quite as pretty as
the boy) could twist
lace & pale blue
ribbons in her curls
& pick wildflowers
& pour out her heart
in an ode no longer
than a lipstick tube.

THE AMAZING CRISWELL

was flamboyant, with spit-curled hair,
a stentorian style of speaking,
and a sequined tuxedo.

He owned a coffin
in which he claimed to sleep.
He grew up in a troubled family
in Indiana with relatives
who owned a funeral home,
and said that he became comfortable
with sleeping in caskets
in the storeroom.

Criswell was known
for his wildly inaccurate predictions.
One was that the city of Denver
would be struck by a ray from space
that would cause all metal

to adopt the qualities of rubber,
leading to horrific accidents
at amusement parks.

He predicted mass cannibalism
and the end of planet Earth,
which he set as happening
on August 18, 1999.

"I had the gift," Criswell once remarked,
"but lost it when I started taking money for it."

DOORBELL

rang in dream.

I half woke: Was it real?

No, it was a dream doorbell.

ORNAMENT

An apple (a pear?)

with holes in it.

Hovering in each hole:

a wasp.

THREE MORE DREAMS

1

Dead nun rising from clogged kitchen sink.

2

"I'm not giving up this dress."

3

Not enough Indians to fight a battle.

SYLVIA PLATH'S
PHONE NUMBERS

Ocean 1212-W
WE5-0219J
Northampton 1700, ext. 293
TRowbridge 6-0848
Cambridge 54589
JU 4-1661
LAfayette 3-2843
PRImrose 9132
North Tawton 370
North Tawton 447

ORANGE BLOOD

The streets of San Francisco
are littered with bodies
of bank robbers & mobsters
prostitutes & pimps

Bullet holes in foreheads

Clothes covered
with that fake orange blood
they used in the seventies

Just pretend dead

No sirens (those will be dubbed in later)

Camera pans
an immaculate city

Mid-morning weekday
only a few tourists about
(everyone else is at work)

Light traffic on bridges

Newly erected Pyramid
dominates the scene

Sky
Maya blue
perpetually wiped clean
by low-flying clouds

Come nightfall
even the junkies
in the Haight
& strippers in North Beach
will have a kind of innocence

Just extras on the set

As close to Utopia
as you could get
in 1973

& now only attainable
in a *Dirty Harry* movie

WONDER WHEEL

I just wanted
to write a poem
with that title.

PAST LIVES

An aviator
who crashed
in the Austrian Alps
Got caught in downdraft
In last moments
mad at myself
I should have known better

An Indian
in the New York area
who wanted to roam
but felt tied
to the tribe
Traveled as far north
as Albany
My name was
Blue Waters Running

A sexually frustrated nun

An Irish boy
who didn't have enough fun

As a Viking
I had to order
someone killed
I didn't want to
but it was expected
of me

An Arab pimp
who abused others

A Jewish boy
who died in the Holocaust

A ship's captain

A rabbi

A witch doctor

There are hundreds more

MERMAIDS

There are many old stories about mermaids.
These stories come from different parts of the world.
There are many pictures of mermaids, too.
But there were never any real mermaids.
Mermaids were supposed to be half maiden and half fish.
They were supposed to live in palaces under the sea.
In the pictures that were drawn of them
they were always beautiful.
In the stories about them they often came out of the sea
to rest on the shore and comb their long golden hair.
P.T. Barnum, the famous circus man, once had
a "mummified mermaid" in an exhibit.
But of course it was a hoax.
The idea of mermaids must have come from something
the people of long ago really saw.
Probably it was some mammal that lives in the sea.
Mammals cannot breathe under water.
They have to come to the top of the water to get air.

Many people think that the mammal that gave people
the idea
of mermaids was a sea cow—
either the manatee or the dugong.
But of course no manatee or dugong ever had long
golden hair!

WHEN BEC SAYS

she's upset
about the way
the market's
behaving
("tragic"),
it calls to mind
the mini-crash
of 1989,
otherwise
known as
"Black Friday,"
and being with
Jimmy in
his room at
the Chelsea
Hotel around
that time and
him saying
something

similar (which
meant he
had money
in the stock
market—
why did that
surprise me)
as he opened
his yellow
file cabinet
(where he
kept his
poems under
lock and key)
to take out
cash for an
afternoon
movie and
early Chinese
dinner on
23rd Street:
"I've been
poor before.

It is not an
experience
I care to
repeat."

THE YOUNG POET

I want what you have
only I want it

now
       when I'm young

not when I'm old

like you

This is
the first poem
I've written
in an Uber car.

in the vitamin section
at Whole Foods.
When the salesgirl
who directed me to that aisle
walks by with another customer,
I say, "I can't find the niacin."
"I'll be right back
to help you," she says.
When she returns
she whispers, "Oh my God,
do you know who that was?"
"Who?"
"Ringo Starr!"
"Cool," I say.
Then: "Did you ask him
for his autograph?"
"No," she says. "I heard
a delivery boy ask him

and he said, 'Please just leave
me alone.'"

This happened in Chicago
on August 11, 2003.

TINY MOSES

on the tiny
frontispiece

of a tiny
bible

made in 1843
for ye

of tiny
belief

1991

I'm sick of Madonna
I'm sick of death
I'm sick of the new R.E.M. album
I'm sick of literary theory
I'm sick of people with no manners
I'm sick of bad poems
I'm sick of *The Simpsons*

THE OLD POET

One more award

before I board

the express

to the posthumous

abyss

(The good news

is there's room

in the pit

for just about

every poet)

♫

Emily – in the Firmament – with Diadems –

Emily – in the Firmament – with Diadems –

Emily – in the Firmament – with Diadems –

Ah –

PHRASES I'VE ORDERED
STRICKEN FROM STUDENT POEMS

my racing heart
muted dreams
sleepless souls
havens of gold
the honey breeze
the trampled moon
under a honey dipped sky
butterfly kisses
the broken goblet of your heart
the endless night
undulating madness
pus-sacks of insanity
the cloistered night
the maze of my fears
the quagmire of hope

THE MAGNIFICENT SEVEN

I fell asleep during the gunfight.

HEARD JUST BEFORE WAKING

"Elizabeth Taylor"

RAISED BY KAREN BLACK

FOR D. A. POWELL

Whenever Daddy went on
    one of his benders,
he'd leave me with his buck-toothed
    paramour,
the "anti-establishment" actress,
    in her Benedict Canyon hippie pad—
the closest thing to home
    in my nomad childhood.

My only toy was her Golden Globe,
    which someone had
dripped with pink candle wax.
    I pretended the Blob
had devoured half the planet—
    by morning the world
would be a ball of chewed
    Bazooka bubble gum.

The Fifty-Foot Woman's huge
        papier-mâché hand,
gigantic ants and tarantulas—
        B-movie monsters were my favorite.
We used to watch such junk
        on *The Late Show*
when she was between parts.

Day and night, her famous friends
        would come and go.
Cher let me try on her purple lipstick.
        Jack Nicholson gave me
my first hit of grass;
        Roman Polanski, my first kiss.

2

ODE TO BUDDY HOLLY

ODE TO BUDDY HOLLY

My first memory
is of an airplane crash.
Two years before yours.
January 31, 1957.
Three and a half, I sat
watching black-
and-white
cartoons while
my mother vacuumed
in another room.
There was a boom;
the house shook.
I remember being dragged
out front and
across a field
toward the disaster.
But how much did I actually see?
It would be years
before I learned what happened:
two planes

collided in the blue
Southern California sky
above Pacoima Junior High
School, where
over two hundred
boys were
ending their
athletic activities
on the playground.
Flaming debris
rained down
on them,
killing three
and injuring
many others,
some critically.
Ritchie Valens
was a student at the school,
but wasn't there
that day
because he was
attending his
grandfather's funeral.

We moved away
several years later
(you were newly dead)
when the Golden State Freeway
was built—the lot
where our house stood
now an off-ramp.
I wouldn't learn your name
until 1971.
Fresh out of
Chatsworth High
and newly eighteen
(and just
beginning
to write),
I heard Don McLean's
"American Pie"
on the radio.
The disc jockey explained
that "The day the music died"
referred to the shock,
a dozen years earlier,
of your sudden death.

From that moment on,
you became
a heroic figure—
random victim
(despite your fame)
of indifferent fate,
the burgeoning artist
cruelly denied
fulfillment
of his gift.

Forty-four
years passed
(fifty-six
since your
tragic crash)
and I was asked
to give a poetry reading
at Texas Tech
University
in Lubbock,
where you were
born and raised.

Newly sixty-two,
I happily
said yes.
And became obsessed,
in the weeks
before my trip,
with your story—
which I'd always
only vaguely known.
On the Internet,
I scrolled
through
the details
of your
accelerated life.
How when you proposed
to your wife,
María Elena,
on your first date
and she suggested
waiting,
you said,
"I don't have time."

How you said
that a lot:
"I don't have time."
How you hardly ever
slept—a trait
common
to those
who die young.
How, newly wed,
you and María Elena
moved into
The Brevoort
at 11 Fifth Avenue,
two blocks north
of Washington Square.
(How many times,
in all my years
in New York,
did I pass
that address,
unaware
that you
once

lived there.)
In apartment 4H,
a matter of days
before
the Winter Dance Party,
you recorded
your last songs—
just you,
your acoustic guitar,
and a tape recorder.
"Peggy Sue
Got Married"
was one of them;
posthumously
released,
studio overdubs
(background
vocals
and additional
instrumentation)
all but
drowned out
your guitar.

The recorder
also captured
three minutes
and twenty-eight seconds
of you and María Elena
talking
and laughing.
(Also sounds
like plates
being put away
in the kitchen.)
The relentless pace
of the tour
and poor
traveling
conditions
(the bus
kept breaking
down
in below-zero
blizzards
as it zigzagged
across the Midwest)

wearied you.
Due to the bus' faulty heater,
your drummer
was hospitalized
with frostbite
and left behind.
Thereafter,
your co-headliner
Ritchie Valens
backed you up
on drums.
By the time
you reached
Clear Lake, Iowa,
a week and a half
into the tour,
you'd had enough.
You chartered
a private plane
to take you
to the next venue
late that night,
right after your show.

A sixteen-year-old girl
from Minnesota
(with a crush
on Ritchie)
took the last known
photo of you:
on stage
at the Surf Ballroom,
pleated curtains
behind you,
teenage admirers
below,
you strum your
1958
Fender Stratocaster
and sing
into the silver mic,
the lenses
of your black-rimmed glasses
(not yet iconic)
glinting
in the camera's flash.

On my Mac,
I looked at black-
and-white pictures
of the charred fuselage
of the small plane,
tangled in barbed wire;
scattered on
the frozen field,
three dark figures,
three young
rock 'n' roll stars—
each hunched facedown
as if trying
to stay warm.
Fine snow
had fallen
after the crash
and drifted
lightly
about the bodies
and wreckage.

I downloaded
and listened to

your hits—
"That'll Be the Day,"
"Oh, Boy!," "Maybe
Baby," "Think It Over,"
"Peggy Sue."
"Rave On,"
with its hiccuppy hook
and manic beat,
a favorite
(fifty-nine plays
on iTunes).

I flew
to Dallas
from Chicago,
changed to
a smaller plane.
Impossible
not to
think of you
on the
brief flight
to Lubbock.

I felt
immediately
at home
in that flat
open
landscape
from which
you sprang
singing
your songs.
The tiny
antiquated
airport
a portal
into the past.
On the way
to the hotel:
cotton fields.
Forever haunted,
those stalks with
their unpicked
tufts of cloud-like
white blooms.

My reading
wasn't until
the following
afternoon;
I had the
morning free.
I'd planned,
in advance,
what I would do.
On a clear, arid
October day,
I drove to your grave.
I had to be there.
Easy to find:
a sign just inside
the cemetery
pointed
to the site.
First row
along the road.
Surrounded
by dry grass.
A flat headstone

engraved
with your name
and dates,
with musical notes
and leaves—
holly leaves,
I realized
later—
and an electric guitar
leaning
against
a Grecian column.
Above,
stuffed
in the sunken vase:
dusty artificial flowers;
gaudy, star-shaped
Happy Birthday
balloon;
weather-beaten
Xeroxed
photograph:
you,

smiling,
in your thick black glasses.
How many
had stood there
like me,
hoping
to sense
your presence.
Or sat
on the flattened
grass
and strummed
your songs.
Some
had left
guitar picks
in the deep-set letters
of your name.
At least
a dozen
of them.
Plastic picks of all colors—
red, yellow, green, blue—

fading in
the intense
West Texas sun.

Your parents,
who stoically
suffered
your loss
into old age,
buried at your side.

Scattered
throughout
the cemetery:
gray and white feathers
(and an occasional
carcass)
of white-winged doves,
killed in the night
by foxes or coyotes
or red-tailed hawks
or feral cats.
Evidence

of fresh death
among the tombstones of
the distantly departed.

It was quiet
and growing hot.
A line of silver grain silos
glinted
in the near distance.

I drove to
the close-by
Buddy Holly
Center
and looked at
the glass cases
full of your
personal effects.
Artifacts that,
arranged
chronologically,
told the story

of your mid-
twentieth-century
American
upbringing.
Childhood
drawings:
cowboy galloping
on stallion,
horses grazing
in a corral.
The Crayolas
you colored
them with—
Burnt Sienna,
Yellow-Green.
Your marbles
and slingshot.
Hunting knives
and rifles.
Your white
high-top
Converse
sneakers

(on which you wrote
your initials
in blue ball-point ink).
White T-shirt
(small) and
denim jacket,
both with "Holly"
written inside
the collar.
Baseball glove.
Report cards.
A pink autograph dog
you signed
"All my love"
on December 28, 1954.
Your yearbooks.
Your camera.
Your collection
of 45s
with songs by
The Everly Brothers
and Ray Charles
and Little Richard

and Bo Diddley
and—a surprise—
Doris Day
on labels
like Domino
and Decca
and Checker
and Roulette.

Then the vestiges
of success.
I stared at
the framed
gold record
of "Peggy Sue."
And at your black-
rimmed glasses,
lensless,
in a glass case of their own.
When your plane
crashed,
they landed
in a snowbank

and weren't discovered
until the spring,
when the snow melted.
They were brought
to the local sheriff's
office, sealed
in a manila envelope,
forgotten
for over
twenty years,
and eventually
found and returned
to María Elena,
who ensured
they were
put on permanent display.

Also in a glass
case of its own,
standing
upright,
your Fender
Stratocaster,

which you last played
less than an hour
before your death.
Three-tone
sunburst
alder body
and maple neck.
The tip of
a white Gibson
guitar pick
wedged
under
the edge
of the plastic
pickguard
(you always
stuck
a spare
pick
there).
The guitar
traveled
in the bus

to your next
engagement,
while you
took to the air.

In the large
last case:
your red
and black
Ariel Cyclone
motorcycle,
purchased
on a lark
in Dallas
after returning
from a tour.
My eye
went right
to the round logo
on the tank:
Ariel.
I thought
of Sylvia Plath

riding a horse
named Ariel
into a flaming sunrise.
I thought of you
riding a bike
named Ariel
on the empty stretch
between
Dallas and Lubbock.
Two artists who
made their mark
and, at the height
of their
creative powers,
quickly disappeared.
I thought
about the years
I've had,
forty more
than you
were permitted,
and what it's taken
for me to fulfill

myself as a poet.
No shooting star
(though I've known
and loved
and lost a few)
impetuously
flashing
toward blackness,
I needed time.
I who thought,
when I was young,
that it might
be better
to die young,
now value
and am thankful for
the time I've been
allowed.
Time to study and learn.
(That never stops.)
Time to suffer
and heal.
(That never

stops, either.)
Time to hoard
and let go.
Time to grow
into and fully
embody my words.

Before leaving
the Buddy Holly Center,
I signed
(with reverence)
the guest book.
In the space
that asked
what brought me
to Lubbock,
I wrote "Poetry."
In the gift shop,
I bought a guitar pick—
white, like
your spare.
I drove back
to the cemetery

and placed it
in the top of
the "E"
in "HOLLEY"
(the true
spelling
of your
last name).
I looked up
at the sky—
wide and untroubled—
Celestial Blue—
with only
a few thin
white streaks
and sweeping "mares' tails"—
strands of wispy cirrus clouds
caused by
ice crystals
in the upper air.

Later, after
my reading,

I was taken up
to the tenth floor
of the architecture
building, for
a Lubbock sunset.
Well worth
the twenty-minute wait
to see the sun,
like a broken egg
yolk, slowly
seep into a
flat, fiery horizon.

The next day
I flew home
(upgraded to first class)
with a check for
two thousand dollars
in my carry-on.
Two thousand dollars—
just for reading
my poems.
But more than money,

Buddy, poetry
made it possible
for me to place
a white guitar pick
on your grave.
May you
never
again travel
without
a spare.

David Trinidad's other books include *Notes on a Past Life* (2016), *Dear Prudence: New and Selected Poems* (2011), and *Peyton Place: A Haiku Soap Opera* (2013). He is also the editor of *A Fast Life: The Collected Poems of Tim Dlugos* (2011). Trinidad lives in Chicago, where he is a Professor of Creative Writing/Poetry at Columbia College.